CROSS-STITCHED WORDS

By Chaitali Sengupta

Setu Publications
PITTSBURGH, USA

Cross-Stitched Words
By

Chaitali Sengupta

Setu Publications
* Pittsburgh, PA (USA) *

© 2021 by Chaitali Sengupta

ISBN-13 (paperback): 978-1-947403-17-8
Cover Designer: Anurag Sharma
Distributed to the book trade worldwide by Setu Publications, Pittsburgh (USA)

All rights reserved. No part of this work may be reproduced, translated, recorded, stored, transmitted, or displayed in any form, or by any means electronic, mechanical, or otherwise without the prior written permission of the author, the copyright owner except for brief quotations in book reviews, and as otherwise permitted by applicable law. Any such quotations must acknowledge the source.

We would be pleased to receive email correspondence regarding this publication or related topics at setuedit@gmail.com.

Although every precaution has been taken in the preparation of this work, neither the author nor the publisher shall have any liability to any person or entity with respect to any loss or damage caused or alleged to be caused directly or indirectly by the information contained in this work.

Setu Literary Publications, Pittsburgh, USA

Cross-Stitched Words

By

Chaitali Sengupta

Acknowledgements

I wish to acknowledge the invaluable assistance of Sunil Sharma, Anurag Sharma and the editors at Setu Publication, Pittsburgh, USA for their care and creativity in shaping up this book.

My special, heartfelt thanks to Dr. Santosh Bakaya, the eminent poet, editor, novelist, essayist who gladly agreed to write a foreword for my book. Your support and help are greatly appreciated, Mam.

I also wish all my friends, for being there with their important inputs, my family members for their patience with me and their continuous encouragement, without which this book would not have seen the light of the day.

CROSS-STITCHED WORDS

Table of Contents

Preface	9
Foreword	11
Desires	17
Tree life	18
Roots	19
Half-stitched heart	20
Green-blue syllables	21
Step Out of Time	22
Deathless in dying	23
Decay	24
Forever is born	25
Lost Freedom	26
Mute land	27
Blood Boots	28
Broken trysts	29
On the pyre of time	30
You never walk alone	31
Silence	32
Autumn	33
Photosynthetic life	34
Trial balance of relations	35
Like a buried dream	36
Nostalgia in a teacup	37
In the dark womb of night	38
Rendezvous of constellations	39
The blood red of birth	40
In the void of eternity	41

Emotions	42
Past	43
Into the vortex	44
Words	45
Death of an age	46
FIRE, the untamed diva	47
Another Ganga	48
A Brief Life	49
In my heart I carry	50
Unspoken words of yours	51
Scars	52
Wintery loneliness	53
Longing	54
Breath	55
Looking back	56
Rootless, as I breathe	57
To last forever	58
A final countdown	59
Betrayals	60
Celestial choreography	61
Author's Bio:	63

Preface

I've loved poetry all my life and I guess it has its roots to all those bedtime 'rhymes' my grandfather engaged me with. However, I was, unfortunately not so finely attuned to his 'rhymes' and 'songs', in which he took almost a childlike pride; my fascination, even then, was with the words. Later, when I published my first poem in The Statesman and The Asian Age, my tryst with words started.

"Cross-Stitched Words" is my first collection of poetry in a prose-poem form, it is a culmination of years of scribbling my thoughts in journals, fed by life experiences. It mourns loss, celebrates Nature, and empowers the readers to seek solace in self-discovery and introspection, reminding them of their moments of personal significance.

In the beginning, I wrote only for myself, as usually is the case. I wrote, as a means of sorting through my thoughts, to remind myself of the various realization, life brought my way. In many ways, it was the only way to quieten down the 'noise' in the mind. It had a strange therapeutic effect, too. But then, slowly, there came a time, when my preoccupation with the words grew. I realized, looking back is also looking inward. I started challenging myself to come out with the 'best' expression that the soul experiences, faced with different situations in our lives. When the words appeared on paper, it was as if, they wrote themselves. The words started influencing me on a deeper level too.

And, when I started sharing my works, at first, with a few trusted friends, they commented positively on my 'unique way of interpreting' life, as it happens to us on this planet. The transition from my 'core fan base' of personal friends to unknown readers, was seamless, thanks to the various, erudite online literary platforms, that welcomed my work with great optimism. Steadily, as my small group of loving readers grew, and I engaged with them, I was surprised to discover their wishes of seeing my works as a collection. This book in your hands is also a result of such ardent wishes.

I'm grateful to have the opportunity to share my words with you. I hope that when you take a page of Cross-Stitched Words, may you find pieces of your own journey in mine, may the "Cross-stitched Words" validate and comfort your feelings. This book is as much yours and it is of life. I thank you immensely, for choosing my words, to spend your time with.

All the best wishes

Chaitali Sengupta

Foreword

While reading the forty-five verses in **Cross-Stitched Words**, I was reminded of a few lines of Erica Jong, *"what makes you a poet is a gift for language, an ability to see into the heart of things, and the ability to deal with important unconscious material ..."*

Well, Chaitali Sengupta is not only a deft wordsmith, with a gift for language, but she also has the knack of looking into the heart of things. Armed with a sensitive quill, she enchants as she goes about celebrating nature, lamenting loss, mourning the curtailment of freedom, ears riveted to the *hissing voice of longings, [Desires]*. Her words become power-packed punches as she writes about the cacophonous *blood boots of tyranny [Blood Boots]* which crush freedom. She pours her anguish about the travails of roots and rootlessness, the pathos of migration, the vicissitudes of life and scars which ooze *blood, with the slightest nudge.*

In the very first poem, *Desires,* her words impress by their intensity, *carving a jagged path through our being.*

Threads of desires stitch the moments of life.
Flame-colored desires
drifting up through a thousand aching fissures in our hearts...
wandering and wending,
 carving a jagged path through our being,
murmuring the tales of yen, glass- crystal;

In *A final countdown*, she paints a very poignant picture of lost love.
Like a trapeze artist overhead,
 waiting for his turn,
love kept waiting and died a slow death...

My favorite in this exquisite collection of poems is, *Lost Freedom*, where the imagery is so powerful that it sears itself in the soul.

When a piece of triangle sunlight
peeped out of the tall building
draping our city,
on a cold winter morning,
they trampled on it,
pinning it under their heavy boots.
Freedom bled
in the tattered field
and blacked out the sun,
while bondage, like a bird
rattled in the cage.

In a similar vein, in another powerful poem, *Blood Boots*, she talks of tyranny brazenly smashing freedom with bloodied boots.

A land beckons through the haze of memories;
our lives ripped apart there,
amidst sepia-toned walls...
where cacophonous blood boots of tyranny,
smashed freedom and a new hatred
was born in the flooding moonlight.
Shivering at their sheer strength I rose,
took my first step,
broke into a run,
in the hungry dark.
I've been running since.
Looking for land for my roots to grow.

The poem, *Unspoken Words of Yours,* appeals by its topicality and by the sensitive way she deals with the plight of the farmers who carry the blood- caked scars of whiplashes on their backs, anguish fallen silent on their parched lips.

Fists once held you down,
to the edge of the very earth you tilled:
pillaged your harvest,
set your ancestral land on fire.
On your backs, the scars of whiplash,
like blood-caked memories of tyranny;
your disembodied voices, pinned to the past.

Turning a philosopher in the poem, *You never walk alone*, she says
You never walk alone;
the pebbles of your lot trudge along,
some scars meet up at the next bend,
summoning the stubborn hills of responsibilities;
and the burden of sorrows,
betrayed by destination, follow on foot.
Sometimes, on the old mission trail,
some good thoughts join in,
carrying the last smiles of the year,
like a fragrance through the air.

In the poem *Rootless, as I breathe…* her pen jabs at the callous indifference of society towards the migrants who sailed over the ghost waters of the Mediterranean, to reach the land of milk and honey and are drowned at sea. Society nonchalantly slurps up the headlines along with the dregs of coffee, while the migrant quietly becomes a small footnote, best ignored.

Words in the morning newspaper,
metallic, scattered, run throughout your city:
it is your oxygen, with your morning coffee;
For you, I'm a headline,
a human-interest story;
For me, a migrant,
the words tell my story.

Brief Life is another poem that *appeals* by its diction and message of transience, the last line leaving a lingering impact:

Life is nothing but a floating,
a slumbering
through the river of time,
diving in like a pilgrim collecting memories like the gems;
resonating briefly like Mozart's symphony through time and space...
and then finally falling awake in a piece of no man's land.

By the time we finish reading her poems, we find ourselves submerged under a cascade of epiphanies, and then when we recover from this cascade, almost magically, we find an almost new world unfurling before us because we have very effortlessly added our own hopes\ wishes \ dreams, to those of the poet, almost believing that there is a world - all healed and recovering from the abysmal depths into which it had fallen.

As I reached the last of her verses, I added my own hope to her heartfelt hope encapsulated in *Celestial Choreography,*

In the season of showers
 Let love pour forth,
sprinkle the heartbeats
 fill it up to the brim;
prune the layers of charred remains into sinless white.
And then, let the sun come up on a cloudless sky,
like a generous lover;
as you open your eyes,
let the planets waltz and align,
in a celestial choreography, creating a constellation in our hearts.

May your hope be answered and may this debut collection of poetry stitch hearts leaving no frayed edges. Because poetry heals in ways we cannot even begin to gauge, and

this book of poetry is indeed a balm for tired souls.
All the best for your future literary pursuits, Chaitali Sengupta.

Dr. Santosh Bakaya

Winner of Reuel International Award [2014] for the long, narrative poem Oh Hark!, Setu Award for excellence [2018] for her 'stellar contribution to world literature', [Setu, bilingual Journal Pittsburgh, USA], the First Keshav Malik Award [2019] for her 'entire staggeringly prolific and quality conscious oeuvre', essayist, poet, novelist, editor, TED x Speaker, Dr. Santosh Bakaya has been acclaimed for her poetic biography of Bapu, *Ballad of Bapu* [Vitasta, Delhi, 2015].

Her latest books:
Only in Darkness can you see the Stars [A Biography of Martin Luther King Jr. Vitasta, 2019]
Songs of Belligerence [2020]
Vodka by the Volga [an E-book - a poetic collaboration with Dr. Koshy, 2020]

Desires

Threads of desire,
stitch the moments of life.
Flame-colored desires,
drifting up, through
a thousand aching fissures
in our hearts,
wandering and wending,
carving a jagged path through our being,
murmuring the tales of yen, glass-crystal;
riddling us, tearing us in two,
until we surrender,
to its hissing voice of longings.

Tree life

There grows within me
the limb of a tree,
spreading its roots,
winding deeper down,
where my yesteryears are buried,
fleeced in moss.
And, my scars come up,
on its aged, wrinkled barks.
Its restless wings, carry my youth,
a time bright green.
And the wind on its branches,
unfastens my late years…
an age passes- or is it a life?
I don't know.

I only know, I gather
the aroma of silence,
dripping off the ragged edges,
under the humming shadows
of my tree life.
There, in the spirit of the woods,
I lower my sorrows.

Roots

Roots, like footnotes on pages
stay underground
amidst dirt and worms,
crawl, spread, in endless intimacy,
in dark silence.

Like words,
connecting the dots,
creating a manuscript of my life,
whispering the tale of my childhood,
sprouting up, like untamed flowers;

sewing the bark of my ancestry
that once murmured resistance,
in a land called genocide.
The one I escaped,
carrying the knotted, tangled roots along.
Those stayed underground
like, footnotes on pages.

Half-stitched heart

When you left,
she stitched her heart shut
with the cord of comforting words;
the needle of her mind
knit an intricate pattern
with unashamed colors, on the tapestry of life
that resembled only you.

With hushed voices, like silk
she carved through days and nights,
every edge of loneliness
with her caring hand.
Sewed the walls tight,
with the thread of forever.

And yet, when years later, again
you spun love,
the stitches frayed;
sputtering from her
half-stitched heart.

Green-blue syllables

From the folds of my sepia pages,
a verse awakes
from her poetic sleep.
Her breath upon my face,
the muse conjures
memories unwanted, long buried.

Like one possessed, she gathers the ageless words,
translucent in a midnight musing,
whispers them to me.
In a mystified trance,
they thrum into life, skillfully forged.

Primordial words, like a painter's brush
paint a Picasso.
Splashing a poetry of
green-blue syllables.

Step Out of Time

Time's currents, silver-eddying,
carry you through rocks and ravines,
rushing head-on, breathless,
as if on a fast lane.

Or, like that tagless luggage,
on a conveyor belt,
circling endlessly,
a waiting game.

On the river of monotony,
life propped up on our elbows sprawl.
Yesterday's regrets taste bitter on our lips,
yet we spin,
at the call of an invisible pendulum,
chiming the theory of
probability and statistics.

Years disappear in meaninglessness,
life, an unending race against clock.
And then, it is time.
To stop the clock; step out of time.

Deathless in dying

Wrapped in warm flannels,
life arrives in November,
with summer's consumed shadows.

Leaves of autumn, like flaming torches,
in a sun bled moment,
traipse in fluid grace,
dropping, like metaphors.

Against the wet bark,
of ripe apple trees,
the moldy mushrooms grow,
like mournful after-thoughts.

Pillowing leaves of gold and russet,
as if, life in a kaleidoscope,
with tints of November,
linger in the frosty network
of our souls,
deathless in dying.

Decay

I separate the shades of past,
searching for my childhood,
spent in a nondescript home.
it stood in a pitiless street,
on life's highway.

On its walls, I scribbled my name,
and let hunger smack and scream
across my face.

I met poverty there, pregnant with need,
her hair unbound,
a shivering soul,
in the dirt and grime.

Years later, I peep inside the house,
carrying now my kitty of plenty and excess.
My hands are now full,
and life, a bright colored topping
on a vanilla ice-cream.

But within the clawing, peeling walls,
I hear the slow footsteps of past.
Rustling there, inside the old trunk,
under the dusty stairway,
my termite-laden childhood lies folded,
betraying my decay.

Forever is born

Sometimes, the words slip
and slide off the mind,
scatter on the floor,
scratch on the paper,
gnaw at our soul
and shiver into meaning.
Then, a poem is born.

Sometimes, the words tilt,
swim in the inkpot,
scratch magic on paper,
combine with our winged dreams,
and flow through us, like rivers.
Then, forever is born.

Lost Freedom

When a piece of triangle sunlight,
peeped out of the tall building
draping our city,
on a cold winter morning,
they trampled on it,
pinning it, under their heavy boots.
Freedom bled
in the tattered field…
and blacked out the sun,
while bondage, like a bird
rattled in the cage.

Measuring the moment
with a spoon, I watched
as no one seemed to mind.
Watching silently, the crumbling of a society...
its last stitch undone.
In the hour of annihilation
my hair stands on end,
words drip
and then fade.

Mute land

In the scrapbook of memories,
I see those red pebbles,
collected beside a river once...
that flew past, in the map of dreams.
There, I suffered with my people
and left in a hurry,
closing the eyes of the dead,
those whom we could not save.

I left...
on the back of my coatless father,
with fire raging in my belly
clutching those red pebbles,
in my hand,
while the mute land stared back at me.

Blood Boots

A land beckons
through the haze of memories.
Our lives ripped apart
there, amidst sepia toned walls...
where cacophonous blood boots
of tyranny,
smashed freedom
and a new hatred was born,
in the flooding moonlight.

Shivering at their sheer strength
I rose, took my first step,
broke into a run,
in the hungry dark.
I've been running since.

Looking for a land
for my roots to grow.

Broken trysts

Pitter-patter, pitter-patter,
are they only drops of rain?
Or the skies
raining memories,
splashing nostalgia,
opening journals
of closed memories...
lone evenings, shared umbrellas,
waiting tram-lines...
broken trysts...
sailing paper boats on lily ponds...
a city drenched,
like a watercolor
on an artist's wall...

On the pyre of time

On the pyre of time,
trust crackles and burns in flames,
and with it burns
a part of me.

Quiet, like the hills,
are the relations today.
You call out loud,
amidst an echoing silence.

Doubts, like knotty strings of jasmine
settle upon the white sheet of
the corpse;

amorphous ego, guides the knife
to draw the battle lines
on the tattered souls;
and all the while, the indifferent ones
with fake smiles of concern,
slice their conscience,
ready their knives
to strike at the relations
yet another time.

You never walk alone

You never walk alone;
the pebbles of your lot trudge along,
some scars meet up at the next bend,
summoning the stubborn hills of responsibilities;
and the burden of sorrows,
betrayed by destination, follow on foot.

Sometimes, on the old mission trail,
some good thoughts
join in,
carrying the last smiles of the year,
like a fragrance through the air.

They come, then leave;
as suddenly as they come.
Yet, I'm not left alone
for I walk
to the song in my heart;
to the caress of the grass
under the detached blue of the sky
with muffled footsteps…

Silence

Silence is
in the beating of your pulse,
in the rising of the sun,
in the dropping of a leaf,
in the flicker of your vein,
in the freezing of the lakes,
in the falling of a star,
in the flowing of your tears,
in the floating of the clouds,
in the stretching of the hills,
in the air in your lungs,
in the subconscious of your soul,
in the passing away of breath,
in the infiniteness of space,
in the nothingness of Shiva.

Autumn

Like that lone leaf
that detaches from a tree,
you leave me.

It is now autumn, in my life.
In the coral light of evening,
miles of silence, stitch to the streets,
that once clung to us, in spring.

Infinite is the distance, now.

Then, time dripped, like the brittle-oak leaves,
twirling on the withered grass.
Then, I carried the sun, in my pocket.

In your absence now
time is like an empty silence,
where untamed memories scream
with no threat of separation,
in the cruel eternity of autumn.

Photosynthetic life

Footsteps of winter
and the stillness it brings,
it goes deeper than in your bones.

The cold burns, crackles, splinters,
life stops, as if in a great pause.
The sleeping planet,
curls up in a fetal position,
in a big sleep, focusing inward,
in the long, dark nights,
on the landscape of our souls.

Winter calls us inside, deep within,
to read our own book of life,
leaving behind the din.

In solid glazed whiteness, like a white quilt,
the snow drapes,
eerie, quiet earth.
On the whited-out planet,
we wait for the
photosynthetic life.

Trial balance of relations

On the crossroads of dialogue,
knitted words
with their silken strands,
draw patterns
with untamed feelings.

Each day creates a tie-dyed moment,
of morphed relationships,
like treasured souvenirs.
They use me up, like an increment, in instalments.

Tattered trust stretches thin,
as new walls come up
drawing more battle lines,
of ego, mistrust, pain.

In the trial balance of relations,
the sum total is only my bleeding heart.

Like a buried dream

Eons ago, in a forgotten age
you had sown the seeds of love;
wrinkled, inside the sinewy womb of earth;
within the heaving cracks,
it lay, pent-up,
wanting nothing, but the ground.

Journeying through time and space
and a thousand galaxies later,
refusing to die,
it swelled, mushroomed.

And one day,
when the slumbering Time, changed its side in sleep,
the molten sun,
smelling like an overripe fruit,
bathed you in swirling gold....

in that quick slip of time,
when you dared to kiss the sunlight,
I blossomed forth,
like a buried dream.

Nostalgia in a teacup

Memories are like
cups of warm tea;
bubbling to the brim,
brewing life.

I sip at it, slowly
relishing, when I am alone.
With the whizz of flavor
ginger, cinnamon, vanilla,
I stir up the past, a rustle of emotions,
swirling with tea and sugar:

milk, like lost promise, drifts out on
pretty porcelain,
and pangs of regret warm against the cup.

Through the rising whiff of vapor,
the sizzling liquid babbles,
it is the past, dear one,
brewing nostalgia in a teacup
to keep you warm.

In the dark womb of night

In the last hours before dawn,
when a pregnant silence reigns
on the vast inky sky,
Earth, with her deep-pooled eyes,
her labored breathing,
watches the darkness
stride forward.

Night, then, is thick, heavy,
like a curtain of sins;
But in the dark womb of
night, the seed takes root,
travels through the soil of our souls,
pushing the sprout towards light;

and Nature, with tears on her dark face,
watches for a new day
to be born out of
the longest night.

Rendezvous of constellations

On the edge of the black velvet sky,
with fistful of yearnings,
the satin-skinned moon,
in its fullness,
cascade through the horizons.

Like, firefly hope,
it quivers and flickers;
and the stars,
like a thousand cross- stitched words,
come out of dotted black holes,
whisper softly,
of past loves
through the souls of time,
spinning starlight of old scars.

And the silvery silence of love,
smile at their gaze,
kiss away their inkiness
caress through their stardust heart;

the planets align, intertwine,
in a rendezvous of constellations,
weaving a fairytale.

The blood red of birth

You're inside me.
Floating, in amniotic fluid,
a dream,
attached umbilically,
to the fathomless fortress within.

A radiant heart,
A sparkling dawn,
A miracle nourished
and cared upon.

Womb-warm, sequestered,
you grew, like the pulse of God;
forging a bond, unknown
that very soon
your life will come undone.

For you, little one,
you're a girl
and you needed to
stay unborn.

Oh, the blessed spark of the Goddess,
force- flushed under my thighs,
you were just a memory then,
a tear pooling in my eyes...

Emptiness comes crashing
on my blackened earth,
the womb remembers forever,
the blood red of birth.

In the void of eternity

Amidst dark waters, tossed by winds and waves,
my humble boat, bobbing up and down,
a dot now, against the endless shore,
where every wave crash, suffer no more.

Caught between the rage,
of a waxing and waning tide,
I try to gather, what can I salvage?

'Return ashore,' whispers the mind.

The shore is distant, a timeless home,
beyond the coastline,
a retreat to origin, of frothy foam.

Like a lonely wanderer I meander,
floundering, wasted,
adrift, on the ocean of consciousness,
forever lost,
in the void of eternity.

Emotions

Eyes wide open,
mind closed shut.
Each relation an act,
a masked procession,
each feeling, with a false face,
guarding, as if a secret affair,
beneath the real skin.

In a shifting, swirling world
of give and take,
emotions are
only a by-product,
seeping into the tear-shaped heart,
setting that chilled-out tone,
on a pasted neutral face,
that sterilizes all feelings.

Past

There, in the distant throngs of solitary trees,
where shadows separate
and the sun-kissed, mustard sun
blaze…
we could have been there.

Together, teeming with our dreams,
nestling beneath the leafy silence....
But now, I know better.

For, you're gone…
and your absence follows me now,
like last summer's fragrance.
And there,
where the mustard sun once blazed,
only yellowing
leaves of autumn,
against a piled up sunless afternoon,
sing the same old song.

Into the vortex

Intimacy, intense though it is,
is measured in spoons.
Alone, on a vast map
charting the black hole of nothingness.

Expanding, until the endless end,
swallowing the light
of the brightest stars.
In severe silence,
harvesting loneliness,
they bask in reflected light.

Or get lost,
deeper into darkness,
of going down,
into the swirling vortex of
cosmic dust.

Words

Words are boundaries,
an edge, a sound.
Silence, a deep space
between the words.

A pause, that holds the chaos.
Awkward, clumsy, wordless,
unspoken, like Nature's
cosmic narration,
at the beginning of space and time.

For, it was
in the womb of silence unblemished,
that feelings rippled,
in measured pulse,
and
words were born.

Death of an age

The trees dropped their tears today,
like burden, heavy and warm
weeping for their roots
gasping, in the bosom of earth.

The rustle of their leaves,
as they fall, like shedding past years,
like a dream gone wrong.

Their tender barks, like morals
shredded to scraps, fall upon
the lap of a broken earth
where only thick silence remains.

The swelling fingers of darkness
stroke her wrinkled face.
Materialism bleach her skin,
a plunderer, cleaving her within,
piercing her, to the marrow.

She endures, brooding like a sage.
In the slits of her eyes
I see, the death of an age.

FIRE, the untamed diva

Fire, the untamed diva in red
gathering her skirt of flames,
saunters towards the nature's stage
to have her last fling.

Warming up to the trees,
with red fire in her eyes,
aroused, fierce, hissing…
she dances in the distance,
over the deep foliage.

Peeking through the trees,
her palms pressing the earth,
she gazes on, a step further
her rhythm steady, her fingers
tracing the world.

Devouring the creatures on run,
the high priestess wails;
lusty, possessed, inhaling smoke
and the hypnotic smell.

Of burnt pines and the battered parks,
Of scarred flowers and charred barks;

Under a black moon,
the silent hills gaze on
a scourged charcoal land;
their hopes pinned on that lone seed
that shall one day
usher in the dawn.

Another Ganga

Another Ganga ....
To sanctify the defiled earth again,
To wash away ages of endless human transgressions.
To endure the burdens of mankind again,
To make it new, to cultivate hope, purging the contamination
Another Ganga....
To rush over the parched and shriveled human mind, sterile conscience, the rot within.
To nourish it back to its inner beauty, a new birthing...
Another Ganga...
To churn out the bedrock of hatred, flush out the roots of evil,
quench the embers of rage, plunging those to her numbing depths...

Let the earth be sanctified again.
Let it go through a cleansing.

A Brief Life

Life is nothing but
a floating
a drifting
a slumbering
through the river of time.
diving in
like a pilgrim
collecting memories
like the gems;
resonating briefly
like Mozart's symphony
through time and space...
and then finally
falling awake
in a piece of no man's land.

In my heart I carry

A certain green patch,
a splash of spring,
a part of forest, in my heart I carry;
to cool off in its shade,
build the nest of my dreams,
in shared solitude.

A handful of beaming sky,
a deeper shade of the yawning heavens, so full of beauty,
in my heart I carry.

To write the dreams,
with the shimmering alphabets
of my blue boundless soul.

Unspoken words of yours

My ancestors,
the toiling sons of soil,
labeled as serfs,
you bargained for a
fistful of wheat
in lieu of your dreams.

Your dreams strapped
like fragile carcasses,
in the field where you bargained them
for the harvest of grains.

The land is green and glossy, now.
Oh, what a rich yield it is…

Fists once held you down,
to the edge
of the very earth you tilled:
pillaged your harvest,
set your ancestral land on fire.

On your backs, the scars of
whiplash,
like blood-caked memories
of tyranny; your disembodied voices,
pinned to the past.

But those unspoken words
of yours,
run silent as blood
through my veins;
one day, I'll pour my heartbeats
into your words.

Scars

Healing one wound,
only to open another…
the soul knows how it was maimed.

It kept the scar,
that spoke its own tales,
taught its own lessons.
Like a half-buried memory,
mapping up to the texture of pain,
marking my identity.

I don't know who you are.
But my wounds, know the sharp-edged touch
of your poking fingers.
And they ooze blood, with the slightest nudge.

Wintery loneliness

Winter has three colors,
gray, black and loneliness;

a frosty loneliness,
sculpts the land white,
dripping cold snowdrifts,
crawl into my skin,
her eyes tightly closed,
she curls up with memories,
that whip at my face, like a bitter gush of wind,
scours my soul, raw-clean.

In the chill of my room,
lay an uneasy, dead quiet,
as the memories
turn into trickling slush,
at my feet
crushed into million pieces,
melting into each other.

The lonely afternoon thaws,
drenches my soul
and washes me away.

Longing

The stories of our lives
like the rains...
an endless drizzling,
creating new alphabets,
new chorus....

each raindrop,
falling in soothing rhythm,
the ups and the downs,
like a beautiful dance...

of resisting and giving in,
of grasping and releasing,
of dissolving and merging,
of holding each moment
like the longing of a
newborn raindrop,
to last forever,
between awake and asleep.

Breath

Happiness slips through grip,
like the thinnest sand,
on the beach of life,
leaving only barbed memories,
in a never-ending spiral.

Yet, we hang on,
like charged particles
in the air.

On the kohled eyelashes,
like silver daydreams, white desires
weigh on…
as long as, breath competes
on the dark chess board,
with life.

Looking back

Looking back, I see the overcrowded past
looping over and over,
trailing like footprints,
on the snow, stamped with regrets,
stuttering, like a garbled echo,
of what could have been.

it takes courage to look back, I say,
at the cozy tricks that time played
and you, tip-toed, sidestepped me,
like the tiny pebbles,
to the chalked other side.
Perhaps gravity drew you there.
Time kept that memory alive.

In the rearview mirror,
wintered memories of past,
mushroom and bulge;

looking forward is uncertain,
and
looking back is looking inward.

Rootless, as I breathe...

Words in the morning newspaper,
metallic, scattered, run throughout your city:
it is your oxygen, with your morning coffee.

For you, I'm a headline, a human-interest story.

For me, a migrant, the words
tell my story.
Of each breath, clenching on
to painful recollection of
unforgiven memories,
as I sailed over the ghost waters
of the Mediterranean, to reach your land
of milk and honey.

Swimming in alphabets
is the tale of that night, where I remember the sea
and those that drowned.

It's my story that I sell,
at your news stand, each morning,
to earn my bread.

You search your moments of glory
in between the lines.

Me, I look for tattered shards of happiness.
Rootless, as I breathe
in between these windowless walls,
pretending to be a princess
wearing a magician's hat,
of discarded old newspapers......

To last forever

A youthful craving to last forever,
an aching addiction to achieve,
to carry the map of success everywhere,
is now a thing of the past.
No such yearning the heart has,
to release.
A bubble life of moments,
sparkling against the dawning rays,
gently bounce, dissolving
in a silent free fall.
In the millennia of existence,
immersed in Time,
mortality sits poised, like a high priest,
sanctioning a settled transaction.

A final countdown

Like that spidery sprig,
above murmuring water,
love kept dangling,
waiting to be plunged,
into the nameless depths.

Like a trapeze artist overhead,
waiting for his turn,
happiness kept waiting
and died a slow death…

Gentle, like the earth on its wobbly axis,
for aeons,
peace kept on revolving,
waiting for a final countdown.

Betrayals

Some scars are necessary
to remember the wounds you gifted.
For, what are wounds
if it gave no scars?

Some pains are necessary
to shape our world.
For, what is pain
if it did not sear your soul?

Some lies, yes, are also necessary
to dismiss the fragile fantasy
of trust...
For, what are lies
if those did not let the truth
bleed-through?

Some betrayals must be there, too,
to shatter the grand illusions.
For, what are betrayals
if it did not bury the tears in your eyes?

Celestial choreography

In the season of showers,
let love pour forth,
sprinkle the heartbeats
fill it up to the brim.

Prune the layers
of charred remains,
into sinless white.
And then,
let the sun come up
on a cloudless sky,
like a generous lover.

As you open your eyes,
let the planets waltz
and align,
in a celestial choreography,
creating a constellation in our hearts.

Author's Bio:

Chaitali Sengupta is a writer and a poet by passion, a financial analyst and a language teacher by profession. She's a translator and a volunteer journalist, based in the Netherlands. Her literary & journalistic articles have appeared in both Dutch and Indian media. A few among those are, *Muse India, Indian Periodical, Howdo, Eindhoven News, NPO.nl, Borderless Journal, Setu Bilingual, The Asian Age, Different Truths, Verse Visual, W-poesis*. Her two translated works include "Quiet Whispers of our Heart" and "A thousand words of heart" (Orange Publishers, 2020 & 2021.) She has co-authored for numerous anthologies, most recent one being the prestigious international anthology *The Kali Project: Invoking the Goddess within, (Indie Blu(e) Publishing, USA),* and *Earth, Fire, Water & Wind* anthology (Authorspress, New Delhi.)

www.ingramcontent.com/pod-product-compliance
Lightning Source LLC
Chambersburg PA
CBHW070633050426
42450CB00011B/3179